Your Book of
Flower Arranging

The YOUR BOOK Series

Summer wild flower arrangement

Your Book of
Flower Arranging

Sheila Macqueen

with drawings by Leslie Marshall and
photographs by Ernest Crowson

FABER & FABER
3 Queen Square London

First published in 1972
by Faber and Faber Limited
3 Queen Square London WCI
Printed in Great Britain by
Latimer Trend & Co Ltd Plymouth

ISBN 0 571 09625 5

Contents

By the same author

Sheila Macqueen's Encyclopaedia of Flower Arranging
Flower Decoration in Churches

Introduction

Flower arranging started a long time ago, and was certainly practised in the eighteenth century, though unfortunately little is known about it. If you can study some old Dutch and Flemish flower paintings you can see the kinds of arrangements that were popular in those days. These pictures will give you a wonderful feeling for flowing line and design, though in practice they are hard to copy as many of the flowers do not grow together at the same time of the year. It is thought that the artist took so long to finish the painting that he had to replace dead flowers with fresh ones, often going through several seasons before the picture was finally completed.

Learning about flower arranging has become very popular with all ages, and if you start when you are young you will enjoy it all your life.

I am sure that many of you love to pick flowers, and I hope that this book will help you to arrange them. I will also tell you how to make flowers last longer once you have picked them, what to look for in the countryside at different times of year, how to make flower or foliage arrangements that will last even through the winter months, and how to make containers from things that can be found about the house.

One point I feel I must stress at the very beginning of this book: never forget that the flowers you need for your arrangements are living and beautiful things and often come from plants that have taken a long time to grow. So please remember a few simple rules. Always cut the flowers, and try not to pull them or break them off: very often the stems do not snap easily and such thoughtless handling can ruin a plant. Always ask permission before picking garden flowers (even from your own parents!) for generally speaking gardeners plant things for the joy of seeing them grow and may not like you to pick their flowers. So ask, just to be on the safe side, and I am quite sure you will be shown many flowers that you can have. You will understand the gardeners' point of view much better when later on, like me, you find you want to grow things for yourself. I always say that I started gardening so that I could cut the flowers and then suddenly I became a gardener and could hardly bear to cut what I had grown!

Aids to Flower Arranging

Before I start on a description of the different arrangements that you can do in each month of the year, I want to talk about various aids to flower arranging, so that when I mention Oasis, for instance, you will have some idea of what to look for. Most of the things listed in this chapter can be bought at a florist's shop, or if your mother is a member of a local flower arranging group, she will be able to get them for you. You should also be able to get them in a large department store.

1. Wire netting

You should get well-galvanized two-inch mesh netting of the sort to be found at any ironmongers. As a guide to the amount you will need for a particular arrangement, measure the aperture of your container and, with florist's scissors or pliers, cut a piece of netting about four or five times

Wire netting

that size. Crush it up so that the holes are a bit uneven and then roll it round in layers and tuck in the ends. Plastic-coated wire from florists is excellent to use in valuable china or glass as it does not rust or scratch, but it is more expensive and is not necessary for everyday use. Once you have got the netting fixed in the container, tie it in place either round the vase or on to the handles with fine wire or string (see 4 and 5 below).

2. Oasis

This is a synthetic green substance that looks a bit like foam rubber. It can be bought in various shapes which can be cut to the size you need to fit any vase. It is most important to soak it well, for if you use Oasis when it is still dry in the middle, obviously your flowers will die from lack of moisture. When you have cut a piece of the size and shape you need (it can be cut easily with a knife) you should place it in a bucket of warm water for at least ten minutes before you start on your arrangement. After

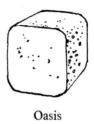

Oasis

a piece of Oasis has been used several times, it tends to break up, so I put two layers of wire netting over the top to hold it in place. Always have two-thirds of the Oasis under the water line and fill up your vase to the very top.

If you should decide not to go on using your Oasis after it has been soaked, you should keep it wet by storing it in a plastic bag, moistening it occasionally until you want to use it again. If it is allowed to dry out, it will not absorb moisture again.

3. Pin-holders

A pin-holder consists of a small round or oblong heavily-weighted metal base into which are set a series of sharp upright spikes: on to these you can press your branch or flower stem at any angle. If you buy pin-holders, in the long run it saves money to choose the best and most expensive, as these are very heavy and usually made of copper. Avoid suction pin-holders. To make a pin-holder yourself, take the lid of a cocoa-tin or any other small shallow lid, and in the centre of it arrange

Pin-holder

tacks or broad-headed thin nails, close together with their points upwards, in a circle or square (you won't need to fill the whole lid unless it is a very small one); then pour in some cement to set them firmly—Polyfilla will do excellently.

Pin-holders can be used in addition to wire netting: they add extra weight to a vase and provide greater security for a really heavy branch or stem, especially in a shallow container. If you use one without netting, roll a piece of plasticine or Bostik No. 5 into a circle and fix it on the base of the pin-holder before putting it in the vase, which at this stage should be absolutely dry as plasticine will not stick on a wet surface.

4. String

Sometimes it is difficult to stop your wire netting from slipping, especially when you start an arrangement. If you thread a piece of string through the top of the netting and tie it round the vase, this will hold the netting in place until you have finished arranging. Then you can cut the string and gently pull out the pieces.

5. Wire

As a general rule I do not think that flowers should be wired, but florist's

Reel of silver wire

wire has several other uses: it is good for splinting bent stems, wiring fruit so that it does not fall off and for use in Christmas decorations. Reels of silver wire are good, for in addition to the uses I have mentioned, being very fine it can be tied round any vase to keep the wire netting firm and has the advantage over string of being more or less invisible so that you need not bother to remove it when the arrangement is complete.

6. Cones or tubes

These are small tin funnel-shaped holders which can be tied to bamboo canes and filled with water. They are really a cheat, making it possible to raise short-stemmed flowers to various heights to suit your arrangement. Attach the cone to the cane with Sellotape.

7. Scissors

Florists' stub scissors are excellent for cutting flower stems and wire. Wilkinson's small secateurs, called Flower Cutters, I find I use more and more, although they are expensive.

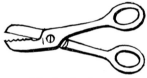

Florists' scissors

8.

For topping up vases you will need a small watering can with a long spout.

Conditioning of the Material

Conditioning is a must. However effective an arrangement may look, it is quite useless if the flowers are not going to last, so treat all your flowers and leaves with great care. Even if you do nothing else, cut soft flower stems at a good slant, since this enables more of the plant cells to be exposed to the water and lets them drink more readily; hammer all woody stems—that is, branches of such plants as lilac and laburnum; and give all flowers a long drink before arranging them. I like to pick my flowers after the heat of the day and leave them overnight in a bucket with the water three-quarters of the way up their stems. If you cannot do this, do try to leave your flowers in deep water for two to three hours before arranging them. It is well worth doing this as one dead flower or leaf can completely spoil the look of a vase.

As you work on an arrangement, remove all leaves that start below the water line. If they are left on the stems they confuse the base of your group and, being partly under water, rot quickly. This not only causes discolouration of the water—it prevents the stems from drinking properly and in consequence the flowers die more quickly. Secondly, remove any unnecessary leaves that obscure the heads of your flowers or berries. This not only helps to show off the flowers better but also enables them to last longer, because only the flower heads and those leaves that are absolutely necessary will have to be supplied with moisture. Never remove all the foliage, however: the odd leaf should be left as it is only the leaves that draw the water up to the flower at the top of the stem.

Some more detailed points are:

Warm water

All cut flowers revive well in warm water, and I use warm water at all times to fill my flower vases. By warm, I mean the temperature at which you can comfortably insert your hand. Flowers that arrive home limp must have their stems cut and placed in warm water and they will revive almost immediately. This method is helpful for:

Sweet William	Aster
Anenome	Canterbury Bell
Marigold	Bluebell (only if on short stem)
Lupin	Daisy family
Delphinium	Queen Anne's Lace
Godetia	Hydrangeas

Boiling water

Unlike warm water which does no harm to stem or leaf, the steam from boiling water can creep up and discolour your stems completely, so this treatment must be given with great care. All you need is about an inch of boiling water in a jug: place just the end of the stem in the water, holding it at an angle so that the steam cannot get at the flower head, leave it till you have counted up to sixty, fill up your jug with cold water and allow your material to have a nice long drink, for several hours if possible. What you are actually doing is expanding the plant cells, dispersing any air bubbles and letting your stem drink freely.

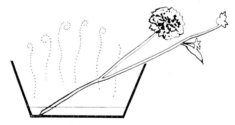

Boiling water treatment

This method is helpful for:
Rose
Dahlia
Poppy
Hollyhock

Wallflower

Phlox

Hellebore (Christmas or Lenten Rose)

Branches of lilac, philadelphus ('syringa'), laburnum, azalea, rhododendron, hydrangea

Any branches of newly-leafing beech, oak etc.

Spraying

If it is possible to spray an arrangement from overhead once you have completed it, this will help your flowers to last very much longer. But don't do it in your living-room!

Starching

A weak solution of starch and water is useful for stiffening very limp leaves and ferns, or for bracken that you may want to press and perhaps gild or paint for Christmas.

To make your solution, add a tablespoonful of starch to two pints of boiling water and when the starch is completely dissolved thin down with

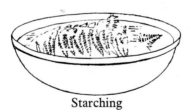

Starching

up to another two pints of cold water. Be careful not to have a solution that is thick and cloggy as this will stick to delicate leaves or ferns. Material should be left overnight in the solution, removed and dried off on layers of newspaper, and then arranged in the ordinary way.

This method is helpful for:

Ferns of all kinds

Arum leaves

Small wild arum in early spring

Branches of maple or other kinds of acer

Submerging

Heads of hydrangea often wilt very quickly when they first come into bloom and I find the only satisfactory way of keeping them is by submerging the heads completely under water. Cut the heads with a small

Submerging

piece of the hard old wood when possible. Dip the cut stems in boiling water and then submerge the head and stem in cold water for a few hours.

Hammering

Hammer any hard woody stem such as branches of apple, beech and indeed all trees.

Other methods

Many people believe that something can be added to the water to prolong the life of the flowers. I am rather uncertain about this, though I have found that liquid Savlon or a very little household bleach keeps the water clear and fresh and I presume must therefore do some good: but be very careful about putting this into a metal container! Add about one table-spoonful to a pint of water.

Most flowers like a little sugar; but if you use this you must put in an aspirin as well: sugar tends to encourage the formation of algae round the stems and the aspirin will counteract this and so allow the stems to drink more freely.

A copper coin is good for chrysanthemums. I find that most flowers last better in a metal container, but this could simply be because the stems are always cool.

All this conditioning may sound a lot of trouble, and many of you may feel that you cannot be bothered. But it is interesting because it is all experimental and some of you may enjoy taking up the challenge of seeing how long you can make things last in water.

Containers

I have deliberately used the word "containers" because, in addition to vases designed for the purpose, there are many other holders that can be used for flower arrangements. Copper pans, pretty teapots, soup plates, sugar bowls, tins painted or covered in paper, casseroles or pyrex dishes: all can be used for holding water and make excellent containers for arranging flowers.

For instance, you can use biscuit tins covered with Japanese wallpaper, as in the picture on page 63, or thick string. Plaited raffia would make another very effective covering, with the plaits sewn together and stuck round the tin. A tin with a hinged lid, all painted red, is ideal for a bunch of anenomes in winter. If your tin will not hold water you may have to put a large jam jar inside it for the water, or you can seal the tin by lighting a candle and letting the melted wax run over the joints.

Half a coconut has a lovely texture that goes well with wild kingcups or buttercups.

A wooden box covered in shells makes a very pretty holder for dried material. Having found a suitable box and collected your shells, wash off all the sea water and dry well and then put small dabs of glue (I use Uhu) on each shell and press well down on to your box. To hold them securely in place cover the shells with Sellotape until the glue has dried.

Many of the arrangements described in this book look particularly good on bases of wood or pressed cork as shown in the drawing here. In these cases any little bowl will do for the water, for it is usually hidden by leaves or can easily be camouflaged by moss or bark.

You may find in your home an urn-shaped vase which is a very good shape for flower arranging. But if you decide to buy a vase, choose an attractive natural colour: pale grey, white, dusty pink or even lilac are all excellent and make it possible to use a wide range of colours in your

20

Various vases and other containers

arrangements. Combinations such as bright red and blue, or red and green, tend to restrain you too much in your choice of flowers. A blue vase filled with flowers in all shades of lilac and blue and perhaps some soft pink gives a lovely feeling of colour flowing from the vase through to the flowers. A scarlet box or vase can add so much intense colour to a mixed red arrangement, but can be used perhaps only once or twice a year.

You can adapt candlesticks for use as containers: at any florist's you can buy a candle cup, a small shallow bowl usually finished in white, gold or silver, with a candle-shaped base that will fit into the socket of your

Wood base and pin-holder

candlestick. These little bowls hold quite a lot of water if used with a round block of Oasis. Fix the candle cup in place with a little plasticine or Bostik No. 5 to stop it slipping out of the candlestick. A word of warning, however: I find these can only be used satisfactorily with heavy or weighted candlesticks, as, with a light candlestick, the weight of the flowers would overbalance the whole thing.

I have a great love for alabaster and have collected it all my life. It has such a warm feeling with its varying tones of cream to deep brown and in some cases almost black. Alabaster vases have become very expensive, but always be on the lookout in a country market or a junk shop as it is still possible to pick up a bargain, and it is such fun having something to look for and collect. In the same way copper, brass, pewter, silver and gilt all give so much choice and so many opportunities, and flowers last particularly well in the coldness of metal. If you are lucky enough to find a bronze container, I am sure that flowers would do well in that too, for I have certainly found that there is some truth in the old wives' tale that an old penny placed in the water will make flowers last better, and this of course is a form of bronze.

Candle cup

Methods of Arrangement

When you are about to arrange a vase of flowers, the first thing to consider is proportion. Be sure that the vase or container you use is suitable for the flowers you have available. Now it can be the other way round: you may have a vase that you particularly want to use, and in that case you must choose the flowers to fit the vase. For instance, if you have lovely long-stemmed gladioli or delphiniums, then the container must be at least half their height—but not *too* large, or you risk getting the unhappy effect shown in the drawing. A few nasturtiums, on the other hand, would look best in a little wineglass like the one in the drawings, or a small pottery bowl about three inches deep.

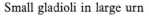

Small gladioli in large urn

Nasturtium arrangement
glass empty and full

Next, you should think about the shape of your arrangement, and here you must be guided by the type of vase and where it is to be placed in the room. The best position is on any surface which is against a plain wall. If your vase is to go in the centre of a table or chest, a traditional fan or triangular arrangement is best suited for this position. A curved or L-shaped design is best on the edge of a shelf or mantelpiece and looks

HOW TO MAKE A FAN-SHAPED ARRANGEMENT

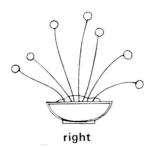

right

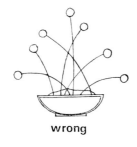

wrong

THE FINISHED ARRANGEMENT

most effective if the high point goes up the side of a mirror or picture as shown in the drawings opposite.

The position you choose will dictate the height you need to fill in the space you have available, but you should never put very tall flowers into a small vase simply in order to attain a certain height.

The traditional or fan-shaped arrangement

Having chosen your vase, put in the Oasis or pin-holder, add and tie in the wire netting, and half-fill with water. Now look at the step-by-step pictures, and you will see that the slender and more pointed stems are placed in position first, the tallest being approximately one-and-a-half or twice the height of the vase. These stems can be slender pointed foliage or flowers like larkspur, gladioli, michaelmas daisy and so on, and should be very firmly anchored in the wire. Next place the stems at the side of the vase: choose ones that are long enough to make the overall width roughly the same as the height, and thus establish your fan. Now fill in the outline with flowers: for the arrangement illustrated, I used delphinium, phlox and scabious, but any delicate and feathery flowers are good. These stems should be placed at angles, like the sticks of an open fan, so that they meet up at the central point which comes below the first and tallest stem that was put in. Be careful to avoid crossed stems. Look at the angle at which the flower has grown and this will help you to choose pieces for the sides of your fan that look as if they are falling naturally. Place one or two pieces so that they come over the edge of the vase in the front: this will help to give a three-dimensional effect.

Lastly, fill in the centre with three or five rounded flowers that have what we call a "face": for example, a dahlia, open rose, chrysanthemum, peony, hydrangea or head of sedum. These flowers should come down the centre of your arrangement, but avoid placing them in a straight line and make each stem a little shorter than the last, until the lowest one, which should have a slightly longer stem allowing you to bring this flowerhead well over the rim of the vase. One or two bold leaves tucked in at the base of the arrangement give undershadow, as in painting.

Finally, fill the vase with water to the very top, and remember to check and add more when necessary.

26

The asymmetrical arrangement

To make an asymmetrical arrangement of the kind I mentioned earlier to stand on a shelf as an outline for a picture, take a low shallow dish and into it put either a pin-holder or some Oasis and three layers of wire netting. Tie this in position with string or wire to hold it firm as shown in the drawing—this is always especially important when you are using a shallow container. Fix your tallest flower into the Oasis or pin-holder placed about three-quarters of the way along on the left, and then thread a longish stem almost horizontally through the netting low on the right. These establish the height and width. Now put in some of the more solid blooms to follow the main line, allowing the lower ones to flow forward. As with the fan-shaped arrangement, add one or two bold leaves and fill in with more stems, always remembering to keep the weight a little more to the left, and using some thinner types of flowers on the right. I tend to work more easily from left to right, as shown in the drawings, but if you want an arrangement to go on the right-hand side of a shelf, then the process is reversed.

How to make an oriental arrangement

The oriental arrangement

Japanese-type flower arrangements have become enormously popular in recent years, and I am sure you will want to try creating oriental arrangements yourself. Simple containers with pin-holders are best for these—perhaps a shallow bowl or paper-covered tin of the kind I have used for the August arrangement on page 63. Fix the pin-holder with a circle of rolled plasticine or Bostik No. 5, and on to it carefully position a branch to make your outline. This can be just a bare well-shaped branch, or one that is lichen-covered or bleached by the sun—again as in the August photograph—which you can look for on the seashore whilst you are on holiday. I have also used branches of burnt gorse, which often have lovely shape and interesting texture. As this is a semi-permanent vase, the shape is all-important. It is vital to fix the branch firmly on to the pin-holder, and if the wood is very hard, it may be necessary to whittle it to a point in order to do this. Once the branch is anchored, add some fresh flowers or leaves. I find that an odd number of leaves or flowers look best: for example, three dahlias, five narcissi, three chrysanthemums, five variegated hosta leaves or three lilies. Of course there is no rule about this, and you may find you prefer to use an even number; flower arranging is such an individual thing that you can experiment all the time. However, at the beginning I think you will find it much easier to use an uneven number of flowers.

Start at the top, placing the tallest stem with the smallest flower head, then place the others below, but avoiding a straight line, so that the heaviest flower head is at the rim of your container. Lastly, place one stem into the vase almost at right angles to the rim so that the flower head comes a little forward: this gives a slightly three-dimensional effect. In this kind of arrangement, it is important to place the stems so that all the flowers face you.

Colour in Flower Arranging

In the West we consider the use of colour an essential part of our flower arranging—indeed I would almost go so far as to say the most important part. However, in the East, in Japan, where they have the longest history of flower arranging in the world, they are much more concerned with line or design. Of course we want to have a good line as well, but they really do not bother about colour to any extent.

One good way of using colour is to make an arrangement that blends with your room, picking up the colours of a cushion, carpet, chair covers or even a picture.

Try arranging a vase of flowers under a painting, a sea picture for instance: search for all the blue-grey and green foliages that blend with the colours of the sea, add a touch of white to represent the foam, and you will be amazed how well this can look.

You can also pick up just one colour in a painting, say the red; or even make a black and white arrangement with black ivy berries and white flowers if you should happen to have a drawing of a black horse, dog or cat, or even a painting of a Puritan gentleman in black gown and white collar. Linking your arrangements with pictures in this way will give you so many ideas and is an exciting way to start training your eye to appreciate colour.

Another idea is to add fruit to your arrangement when it is to be placed below a still-life painting.

If you use colour in the ways that I have described, you will be surprised how often someone will say immediately how nice your red dahlias look with the red books, or cushions, and so on, and this is the nicest thing that can happen. You have achieved the highest compliment: you have made your flowers part of the room, drawing attention to something of far greater value.

29

Wild Flowers

>>>

"Wild" is a poor description because flowers that are wild in one part of the world are often much sought after in other countries. Perhaps just because they grow so easily they do not get the respect they deserve. To give you an example, our so-called cow parsley which grows along our hedgerows in June is something that every bride in the Pacific Islands would like to have in her bridal bouquet. Kalmia, a shrub which I have such difficulty in growing here, grows wild on the hills in Virginia and in mid-May the hillsides are pink with its delightful flowers.

In this country we are still allowed to pick our native or wild flowers: people in many other countries are not so fortunate, for their native plants are protected, and anyone found picking the rarer ones indiscriminately may be heavily fined. However, as a result of our more easy going ways, many wild orchids and fritillaries have disappeared for ever from our banks and fields because people not only picked the flowers but dug up whole plants. Sadly, these wild flowers will not survive in a domestic garden, I think usually because the plant was taken up when in flower and few growing things can survive such treatment, especially since we can never give them the right conditions in our own gardens.

Just because we are allowed to pick primroses, branches of pussy willow, catkins, bluebells and cow parsley, please remember to pick with real care. Always take scissors or better still pruners if you want to cut branches—you may have noticed that willow branches, for instance, do not break off cleanly and you end up with a jagged branch torn from the tree and causing a great deal of damage. Bluebells must be picked with very short stems or they will not last long. Never pull bluebells with that piece of white stem, for this all needs to go back into the bulb for another year. Best of all, when collecting wild flowers take along a largish polythene bag. There are always plenty of these about nowadays, and if you put your flowers into them as they are picked there is a good chance that your primroses and bluebells will still be alive and quite fresh when you get them home. For primroses, if you take little elastic bands and pop one round each bunch as you pick it, the flowers will be all ready to arrange.

January

A difficult month for flowers. With Christmas over and all the evergreen decorations on the bonfire, one longs most of all for something fresh.

Daffodils are so beautiful and give a feeling that spring cannot be far away. If you can possibly afford it, buy a bunch and try arranging the flowers in a shallow dish with a branch of hazel (this should just be forming its catkins) using a layer of moss to cover the wire netting. Moss may be difficult to find when there is snow, but if, earlier in the winter, you remember to collect any you see on a roof or wall and put it into a polythene bag, you will have a supply for several weeks. Alternatively, you can buy reindeer moss at a florist's shop, and though this looks very grey and dry, it becomes soft and attractive when wet. If you cannot get any kind of moss, use a pin-holder, and cover with pebbles, or a piece of bark. Daffodils last well in shallow water, so an arrangement of this kind will stay fresh for quite a long time. Add a stem of variegated laurel, three bergenia leaves, a head of green hellebore (Lenten Rose), a stem of shiny camellia foliage, or even pieces of curly kale, and you will be surprised how this brings your vase to life.

Arrangement for January

Dried ferns used as a background can also make a few daffodils look very important, especially if they are arranged with one or two bergenia leaves at the bottom of the container, as shown by the drawings.

Method: For a vase like the one in the drawing, fill a shallow oblong dish with crushed-up two-inch mesh wire netting, kept in place with a piece of string. You will have to add water because of the fresh material, and this will cause the stems of the dried pieces to go soft in time, but they

32

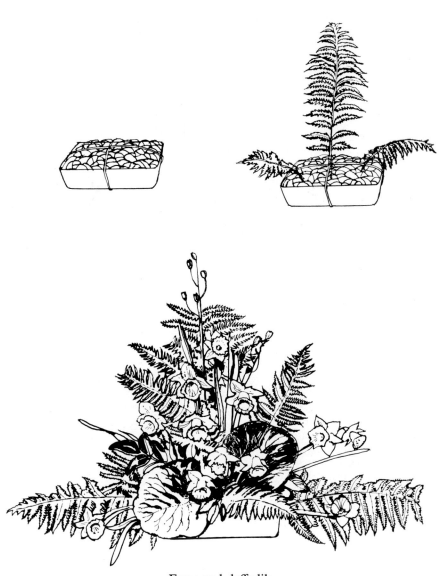

Ferns and daffodils

will remain quite unharmed otherwise. Make the outline shape with bracken as shown, then add the solid leaves of bergenia and lastly place the daffodils and their leaf spikes. The dish in the illustration was pale yellow, to pick up the colour of the flowers and give a nice blending effect.

Try to find some trails of ivy that have taken on attractive shapes and use these in a vase during January: they will give you a wonderful chance of learning to make a good design. A wall-vase of ivy can look particularly effective. Small pieces of yellow variegated ivy help to add lightness to any vase. Ivy will last very much better if you hammer the stems well and leave them submerged in a bath or sink of cold water overnight; then before arranging, shake them well and dry carefully.

Mixed greens in January are a little difficult, but you may be able to

Various carnation arrangements

34

find ivy, bergenia, laurel, dried bracken and a few good-shaped bare branches of elm or oak, for instance, which often have well-shaped branches. Your vase may have very little colour variation at this time of year, but different textures are important too.

Carnations are such a useful flower because they are available all the year round. They are cheapest to buy in August, but they are most treasured in winter, and I can think of a number of ways in which you can make the most of a dozen carnations. Many people feel that these flowers are very difficult to arrange, and rather sadly they are one of the few flowers that really do live much longer in water if they are placed in a vase quite alone, and without any unrelated foliage. Therefore if you can find some of their own leaves this is possibly the best way to use them. However, one can scarcely ever do this, especially when they are bought flowers, and personally I find that carnations look so much nicer arranged with blossom, or a branch, or perhaps a few grey leaves, that it is worth shortening their lives a little. You can see from the illustration how many simple ways there are of using them, varying from an arrange- ment of three flowers with a beautiful branch of contorted hazel, to two in a small cigarette box. The goblet is modern white milk glass filled with wire netting; in it seven carnations are arranged with a background of prunus. An uneven number of flowers is often easier to arrange as it helps you to avoid too many straight lines.

Idea for the month

Bring into the house some branches of forsythia or flowering currant, hammer the stems well, keep in water in a warm place and watch the buds opening. You can help to speed up the process by keeping the vase topped up with warm water, or by changing the water frequently. It generally takes from four to five weeks from bud to flower, and the branches can then be used in your arrangements.

February

You might be lucky enough to find snowdrops flowering in your garden this month; if not, perhaps you can buy a bunch for an egg-cup like the little arrangement shown here. I suggest that you use an egg-cup because these tiny flowers can look quite lost in any normal vase, however small, giving the effect shown in this drawing. For my arrangement, the egg-cup was filled with wire netting covered with some moss which I found in a corner where nettles were coming up: you can often find moss on a patch of waste ground. Snowdrops are at their best arranged like this, with only one or two of their own leaves, for it gives you a chance to see the beauty of every little bell and the underskirt of each flower tipped with brilliant green.

Snowdrops in over-large
vase

Snowdrops in eggcup

36

Another way of using snowdrops is to make a miniature garden. A bed of moss in a shallow dish like the one in the drawing—a soup plate would do very well—makes the ground. Into this you cluster small bunches of

Moss garden

snowdrops, crocus, grape hyacinths, scilla, primroses—in fact, little clumps of any of the early short-stemmed flowers.

Arrangement for February

Another idea is to make a planted garden. Small plants suitable for this are very popular and can be bought not only at florists' shops, but also in supermarkets and Woolworths.

Method: Choose three or four good plants of different heights, get a shallow dish—preferably an oval meat dish—and fill it with best soil. Then find some pretty stones to use as rocks, or a moss-covered piece of branch which can be a log, small pebbles or bits of broken flower pot for your path, and perhaps even an old handbag mirror to make a pond. You can have a lot of fun planning your little garden, for instance by making the soil higher in one place as shown in the drawing, to give a more interesting effect. When the "ground" has been created, unpot your plants and place them in position. Move them around until you are satisfied with the effect, then make holes in the soil and plant them, being

37

Planted garden

sure to spread out their roots well. Press the plants very firmly into the soil—otherwise they won't grow—and water the garden as soon as you have finished making it. These gardens like overhead spraying: every few days place the dish on a draining board and spray the plants from a watering can or splash them with cold water from a nail brush shaken over their heads. Then dry the dish and stand it on a mat for a while to drain. As a plant or bulb dies you can replace it, but you will find that some of the foliage plants I have suggested will last for months.

Suggested plants for your garden

Flowering plants
Crocus
Polyanthus
Coloured primroses
Cyclamen
Primula
Hyacinth

Foliage plants
Striped green leaf of
    Chlorophytum (Spider Plant)
Peperomia (Pepper Elder)
Ivy
Begonia
Tradescantia (Wandering Jew)
Ferns

Anemones can be bought in February, and if you can find a small toffee tin with a hinged lid, you could try painting it and using it for one or two bunches of anemones. Find out first whether the tin holds water; if not, use a little dish placed inside it for the water, or seal the tin by melting a candle and letting the wax run over the joints to make them watertight. Red is the best colour for a container for these little flowers as it makes them look so much more important and gives them the chance of showing all their lovely colours. Do not put in any green as it takes away from the colour effect giving a red and green arrangement rather than just a concentration of reds.

Conditioning note: As soon as you get the anemones home, cut off the base of the stems and place the flowers in warm water for an hour or two before arranging: this will help them to last longer. If by any chance you can use Lenten Roses or hellebores which flower at this time of the year, after cutting them, take a pin and scratch a line right down the stem from the flower head and then give them a long drink in deep water. This method will lengthen their life in water, although you must not expect them to last very long.

Idea for the month

You might like to grow a little mustard and cress to eat for tea on bread and butter. Buy a packet of mustard and cress seed, cut a piece of flannel the size of a plate and soak it with water, and then scatter the seeds in a layer quite thickly over the flannel. I think you will find that the cress comes up first. When it is ready, cut with a pair of scissors and start your growing again on a new piece of flannel. Always keep the flannel wet.

March

As flowers are still scarce in the garden and expensive to buy, you might like to try making an oriental-type arrangement with just a bare branch and a few iris or tulips in a shallow dish. Use a pin-holder placed to one side of the dish (see page 27), fix your branch first, add your iris and then cover the pin-holder with a few stones. Good shaped branches may be of oak or gnarled pear or apple, but, best of all, look for branches of alder with catkins. Alders often grow in swampy places or on river banks, and

Basket of primulas

the catkins grow on branches that have last year's cone clusters on as well. Specially grown contorted branches may be of a type of hazel (*Corylus avellana* "Contorta") or willow (*Salix matsudana* "Tortuosa") both of which can have striking shapes, as you can see from the illustration for January, where I have used a branch of contorted hazel with carnations.

Using a basket for spring flowers always helps to make them look unsophisticated and happy. Take any shallow basket and use a Pyrex pie dish to hold the water—you do not need an expensive tin liner. In the arrangement shown in the drawing I have used a mass of polyanthus,

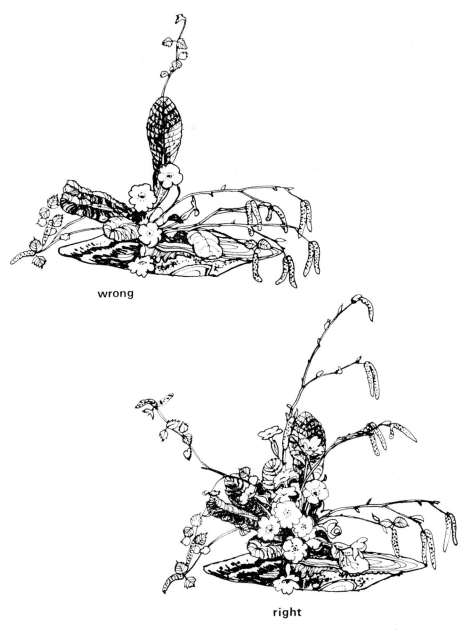

wrong

right

Right and wrong way to arrange alder and primulas on wood

putting several stems of one colour together so as to get a better effect: group the yellows and white flowers, the blues and pinks, and so on. Before arranging them, with a pin prick right through the stem of each flower, just below the flower head, and then allow them a nice long drink in warm water up to their necks for a few hours. This may sound an awful nuisance, but it is worth it because the flowers really will last without drooping.

Arrangement for March

For the arrangement shown in the drawings I used a small branch of catkin with a few coloured primroses on a piece of wood.

Method: Cut a slanting slice of silver birch about two inches thick, making an oval base (you will probably have to get one of your parents to help you with this). On the wood, place as shown in the drawing on page 21 a shallow bowl containing a pin-holder and crushed-up wire netting, which I camouflaged with a piece of moss—but bark would do equally well.

When placing your branch and flowers, do not attempt to make a symmetrical arrangement—you can see from the drawing how wrong that looks. Instead, follow the simple rules I mentioned earlier on page 27 (asymmetrical arrangement). Again, the drawings will I think help you more than any description.

Idea for the month

Look in the shops for seeds of annuals so that you can plant some now for cutting in midsummer. Here are some suggestions:

Godetia: single or double.

Clarkia: lovely range of colour from pink to red, excellent for cutting but use only when fully open well up the stem. If left in water, clarkias dry well for winter use.

Pot Marigold (Calendula): yellow and orange.

Sweet William: excellent for cutting and arranging. The seeds ought really to be sown in May to bloom the following year.

42

Nasturtium: the Gold Gleam hybrids give a lovely choice of colour from pale cream to almost brown, orange and scarlet.

Larkspur: again, these last well if picked when open right up the stem, and are excellent for winter use if allowed to remain in water in a warm place until really dry.

Aster: many new American hybrid varieties giving a wide choice of colour in pink and mauve. Single and double flowers.

All these seeds can be sown out of doors in ground where they are to stay and thinned out to six or nine inches apart.

For some more unusual plants for decoration, you will have to order the seeds from a specialist grower (see note on page 85). These could include:

Amaranthus (Love-lies-bleeding): the green variety (*A. alba*) is particularly good. If the seeds are sown in March in a greenhouse, they should be transplanted to the garden in May or June.

Atriplex: a red foliage looking rather like beet or dock in seed. It seeds itself, is lovely at any time and dries well.

Euphorbia marginata (Snow-on-the-mountain): green and white leaf bracts that look like flowers.

Alchemilla mollis (Ladies' Mantle): herbaceous perennial with feathery lime-green flowers and beautiful leaves. It is very well worth growing and you will have it always as it seeds itself everywhere.

Green Tobacco (*Nicotiana alata*): lime-green flowers of excellent blending colour.

Angelica: a herb of which the candied stem is used for decoration on trifles and cakes. I use it for the finely-shaped leaves which often turn gold. A good seed head to dry for winter.

April

Now you can use forsythia cut straight from the garden, hammering the stems to make the branches last longer in water. To me nothing looks nicer than a mass of golden forsythia and yellow daffodils. As they are so plentiful in the garden and inexpensive to buy, make the most of them: fill a copper pan or basket and enjoy the feeling of spring and the cheerful effect they will give you.

All the early spring bulbs—baby narcissi, grape hyacinths, Glory of the Snow and, later, primroses, polyanthas, primulas and pansies—look delightful arranged in posies in a china cup. Try to pick up the colouring of the china in your flowers. The photograph shows a cup filled with summer flowers, but I have included it here so that I can tell you how to make this little arrangement with all the early spring flowers you can find in April.

First tilt the cup so that it rests on its handle—to prevent it from falling over—and put into it a little piece of soaked Oasis. This will probably have to be held in place by wire netting, the snag ends of which should be bent over the rim of the cup in a couple of places, and possibly round the handle too. The cup is then ready to be filled with primroses or any other suitable little pieces from the garden. Don't forget to position one or two flowers so as to hide the wire round the handle.

Arrangement for April

Another idea on similar lines, also using something that you all have in the house, is a posy on a large plate. In the one shown here, I followed the blue and white pattern on the china by using grape hyacinths, blue violas and a few white violets which are very attractive, but have no scent.

Arrangement in cup and saucer

Method: The first drawing shows you the base from which to start. As you will see, I used a small brick of well-soaked Oasis measuring about three inches square, and covered by a layer of two-inch mesh wire

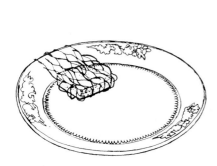

Oasis block wired to plate

Posy on plate

netting, hooked round the rim of the plate to hold it steady. (It might be best to use a plastic-coated netting for this arrangement, so as to be sure that the plate will not get scratched.) The little flowers go into the Oasis until it is completely covered, as you can see from the second drawing. For this type of arrangement you should try to put one or two flowers of the same colour together, thus emphasizing the colouring of the china.

At this time of year you may also see a stately flower growing, especially in old or cottage gardens—this is the Crown Imperial Lily (*Fritillaria imperialis*), which grows on a long straight stem about two feet tall and has a head of multiple pendulant bells in yellow or bronze, a strange aromatic perfume and a tuft of green leaves coming out of the head at the top rather like a pineapple. There is such a sweet story about this flower that I feel I must tell it to you. It is said that when Christ walked in the Garden of Gethsemane that Eastertide many years ago, the crown imperial lilies proudly held up their heads, but ever since have felt humbled and ashamed and now hang their heads with a teardrop in each eye. The teardrop is there to be seen if you invert the delicate bell-shaped flowers.

Ideas for the month

Sow some seeds of decorative kale or cabbage—you can order a packet from any good seedsman (see page 85). These plants are wonderful to pick in the autumn, using either small leaves or one enormous head.

If you would like to have some early gladioli, plant a few now. Never plant a lot of gladioli at once: if you plant a few corms every fortnight you will have some flowers ready to cut for weeks on end through the summer.

Another idea for this month, if you live anywhere near wide open spaces or the sea, is to look on the headlands which are often golden with gorse—but remember to wear strong gloves when picking it. Arranged in a wooden or brass bowl, you will get a glowing mass.

May

Suddenly in May we get a wealth of colour in the garden and so much from which to choose. Everything bursts into bloom and it is without doubt one of the loveliest months of the year for the flower arranger: wild cherry in the hedges, azaleas and rhododendron, late tulips and woods of bluebells. If you pick bluebells cut them with stems about three or four inches long at the most, and pack them tightly together in a tin or bowl. Cow parsley—which you may call Queen Anne's Lace—will soon be out, and this very delicate flower looks lovely arranged in glass. It is always advisable to pick it the day before you arrange it and give it a good soak all night in deep water.

Another wild flower seen in the countryside at this time of year is the white dead nettle: if you remove all the leaves, these look very pretty and last a long time in water. Keep your eyes open too for the leaves and flowers of the wild arum. I find that the leaves last very much better if they are put into starch water (see page 17) and allowed to soak overnight before being used.

Ideas for the month

May is the month of our Chelsea Flower Show, undoubtedly one of the greatest in the world. So I am going to give you some ideas that you might like to try for your local flower show.

The drawing shows you the front of a little house: copy this—or a house front of your own design—on to stiff card, and make a garden to go in front of it. I first saw this done in Canada, where the gardens were made in sand on baking trays. The first prize winner had made a path out of tea leaves and her grass lawn from chopped chives (in Canada there is no grass in winter!). Small stones represented a rock garden, a bare branch was used for a deciduous tree, pieces of conifers as pine trees, and so on.

The winning house and garden

The same Canadian flower show had a class of pressed and dried flowers called 'Cut and Dried'. Pressed flowers in the form of a picture are so very much more interesting than stuck in a book, so I hope the following suggestion will give you some ideas for children's classes in your local flower show.

Pressed flowers

Place your flowers between blotting paper, which should be changed every day for best result. Don't throw away the damp paper: if you allow it to dry, you can use it over and over again. Press only a few flowers at the same time. Newspapers can also be used successfully. Violas and pansies press very well, as do Queen Anne's Lace, grasses and small coloured leaves. Avoid roses and all hard-centred flowers such as dahlias. Place each flower very carefully, because if a petal gets bent it will be very noticeable in your final arrangement, and then lay your blotting paper under a pile of heavy books. The amount of time needed for the drying process will, of course, vary with the thickness of the flower head: take a peep at them after about seven days to see whether they are ready. You will soon learn to tell whether they are dry from their slightly brittle appearance.

For mounting the flowers, try to find a piece of coloured paper, which will show them off much better than plain white. Choose your pieces with care—not too many or the result will look overcrowded—and arrange them on the paper until you are satisfied with the effect. A little nosegay of mixed flowers and grasses looks well, and so does a simple spray using, for instance, only the flowers and leaves of Queen Anne's Lace. When you are happy with the effect, carefully spread a very little Uhu gum on the back of each flower and press lightly in place again with your fingers. Cover the mounted flowers with cellophane or a transparent plastic film, which can simply be Sellotaped on to the back of the mounting paper, or finished off with an edge of coloured or shiny tape.

Later in the year, I will give you some more ideas for using these pressed flowers for making Christmas presents, so remember to go on with your pressing throughout the summer.

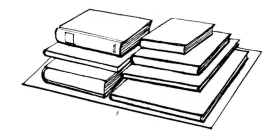

June

⤜⤜⤜

Flaming June as it is sometimes called is a lovely time for flowers: a month when the first of my adored roses bloom, when the honeysuckle scents the evening air and climbs with gay abandon over cottage walls, when pinks, mock orange, lavender and so many other sweet-scented flowers appear.

This is a time of soft colours, giving you a chance to pick pale pink peonies and lime tree branches coming into flower; or for making vases of strong colours, reds in all shades, flame and apricot. In fact June is almost the one month of the year when you can do any colour scheme that you wish.

You will see in the pages of this book some arrangements using roses. One in particular is interesting because of the background. I had these two photographs taken to show you the importance of positioning a vase: you will see that a pleasing vase looks completely different against the confusion of wallpaper—though of course if the colouring were right this could look very effective. However, you will notice how very much better the flowers stand out when the vase is placed against a plain background.

The conditioning of roses is important. I find it best if the ends of the stems are placed in about an inch of boiling water for about a minute (holding the stems at an angle so that the steam does not hurt the flower-heads, or your fingers) and the jug then filled with cold water. The flowers should be left in this for a good long drink, at least two hours, before arranging.

If you pick flowering branches of lime in June, remove all the leaves as soon as possible. In this way you stop dehydration, and the flowers have a much better chance of survival. You can go on picking lime flowers for several months after they first appear, even when they form seed heads; and also don't forget that they take up glycerine very well

Same vase of roses against
two different backgrounds

(see page 58) especially if the branches are picked just before the flower actually opens. So lime can be used through June, July, August and September.

Arrangement for June

The dining-table arrangement shown in the illustrations is naturally an all-round arrangement, and the photographs show you three stages in doing this.

Method: After preparing your vase in the usual way with Oasis and wire netting held in position with string, first make the outline of your arrangement, pushing stems into position along the rim of the bowl. It is important that these should go in first so that you can see that the stems are actually in the water. The next step is to place the central flower dead in the middle of your bowl, and as tall as you are going to make the arrangement. Now you are at the stage shown in the first illustration. Then place one or two short stems just above the rim of the

Stages in making a table centre arrangement

vase, and from here gradually fill in. The arrangement in the picture
happens to be in shades of pink, and to help the shape I have put in
one or two flowers of the same variety together. If, on the other hand,
you are using flowers in mixed colours, then place one or two of the
same colour together in small clusters. This gives a much more clear-cut
effect to your arrangement, and prevents a spotty appearance. For a table
centre arrangement, always place each flower so that it is looking at you,
then turn the bowl and work on the next section. Try as you may, you
will never have every side identical, but aim for a good balance and
general effect. It is cheering to remember that you cannot see both sides
at once!

Idea for the month

As I talked earlier of sweet scents, I thought that those of you who have
gardens might like to try making some pot-pourri, that sweetly-scented
mixture of dried flowers and leaves. The chief ingredient is rose petals:
the roses for these should be picked fresh and left to dry, outside if you
like but not in full sun. Next mix 1 lb. rough salt with 3 oz. saltpetre
(halve these quantities if you don't want to make a lot). Then into a
stone jar put alternate handfuls of petals and salt, cover the jar tightly
and leave until you have collected more, adding them in layers with the
salt as shown in the drawing until you have used all your salt mixture.
In a second jar mix the ingredients for the scent. I will give you the
best recipe I know, but it is a little extravagant, and if you use just two
of the oils, I think you will still find that it is very good. As with the
saltpetre, you can buy the ingredients from any large branch of Boots
the chemists.

    1 oz. each of cinnamon, allspice and ground nutmeg
    4 oz. powdered orris root
    $\frac{1}{2}$ oz. of oils of bergamot, geranium, oil of lavender
    the juice and finely chopped rind of 3 lemons

Mix all these together and then add them to your rose-petal and salt
mixture, stirring in well. As the summer goes on, put in dried flowers
of lavender, clove pinks, violets and philadelphus; and leaves of sweet
verbena, bergamot, sweet bay, thyme, mint and any other sweet-scented

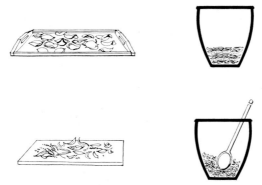

Stages in making pot-pourri

leaves or flowers you may have in your garden, adding each as they come into flower. Remember to stir the mixture every day. For added colour try to get some red rose petals, delphinium and petunias.

When your pot-pourri is ready, after the summer is over, put it into a bowl and it will give a lovely scent, and for years after you have made it, you can run your hands through it to release the perfumes. It is often used also for filling sachets of muslin to put in your drawers or cupboards.

July

Lilies at once come to mind as the best flower this month: *Lilium auratum*, better known as the sun lily of Japan; *L. regale*, with its sweet-scented cream petals backed with pale pink; the common tiger lily in brilliant orange, and some of the superb De Graaff lilies, ranging from a clear yellow, called Limelight, to cream and orange. Their grower is a Dutchman who settled in the U.S.A. and has spent a lifetime on hybridizing; the naturally well-drained soil of Oregon seems to have provided him with ideal conditions. If you can possibly do so, you will find that lilies are worth all the trouble you put into making them grow, but now, of course, we are fortunate in being able to buy them more easily than ever before in our flower markets. Whether picked or bought, I find they require little special attention when cut, though I do like to give them one night in deep water before arranging them.

July is the ideal month for very large groups of flowers, suitable for church weddings and parties, and if the season is right, this is the one time of year when you can make a really big pure white group. Take sprays of philadelphus (mock orange), remove all the leaves as for lime branches (see page 50), and add stems of white delphiniums, white peonies and white lilies. Not only will you have a perfect wedding group if you are placing it in a church, but if you put it in your home you will find that it scents the whole house. Do remember to check it regularly and frequently for water, for it is surprising how quickly the water level can drop in these huge groups, especially in the first twenty-four hours.

July is a good month for making a pyramid of roses—floribunda or rambler are best for this. Make a cone of small-mesh wire as shown in the drawing. Fill with crushed Oasis (I keep a polythene bag for all my old and broken bits of Oasis, just for this purpose) and leave to soak

56

Making and covering wire cone

in water for an hour. Then cover the cone with the piece of kitchen foil, which keeps in the moisture. Place your cone in an urn-type vase and press into place the short-stemmed roses of your choice. The method can also be used for hydrangea heads and later in the year for dahlias.

Arrangement for July

This month the hedgerows are full of interest. Look for instance for the leaves of cow parsley and hemlock, both of which often take on good colour in July, and for docks turning from green to brown. Bulrushes can be found in the ponds, and while you are there look to see if you can find some green seed heads of the wild yellow pond iris. You can use some of these in arrangements this month and hang the rest upside down to dry and use in winter.

A lovely arrangement using many wild flowers can be made with a flat basketwork tray as base (see the colour illustration facing the title page).

Method: On the tray put a shallow ovenware bowl, with a pin-holder and crushed-up wire netting (or you can use Oasis). Fill the bowl with water and place the tallest stems in position three-quarters of the way back in the bowl; then place the side pieces to give you the outline; and finally fill in the centre with some of the bolder material, always bearing in mind that the flowers with a face make the best focal point.

Idea for the month

This must surely be drying and preserving. Try glycerining branches of beech now. The general tendency is to leave this until the autumn, but by then the sap is no longer rising, and this must naturally help the plant to take up the glycerine. Look at the illustration and if possible choose an upright jar like the one in the drawing rather than an open vase for the mixture. Take one part of glycerine and two parts of hot

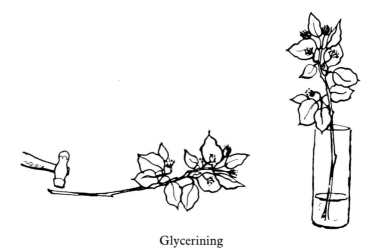

Glycerining

water and mix well. Hammer the ends of the stems and place them in the solution making sure that the glycerine comes about two inches up the stems. Now there are two definite schools of thought about this, one suggesting that the branches need a night in deep water before glycerining and the second, which I am inclined to follow, believing it better to put the stems straight into the mixture. I only put the branches in water if they have flagged a little in transit. After about ten days you may find

JULY

that you need to add more water to your glycerine. Stems of laurel and other evergreens can be done in the same way later in the year.

Suggestions for glycerining:

Beech sprays	Lime flowers
Berries	Sweet chestnut
Laurel	Old man's beard
Saxifrage	Hornbeam
Viburnum	Molucella flower

Do experiment with other things, but remember that generally speaking soft tender leaves like maples are not good subjects for glycerining.

August

Annuals, if you grow them, are at their best this month. Antirrhinums, marigolds, petunias (these last very much better as a cut flower than is generally appreciated), godetias, dahlias and gladioli all give a wealth of colour.

But August is also a good time of year for doing mixed greens. These green arrangements are so cool and effective and are possibly my most favourite arrangement—if one can really say that! You can use green seed heads of lupin, lilies, iris, green tobacco, molucella (Bells of Ireland) and green sedum before it has turned red; and add sprays of golden privet, variegated weigela and green rose plantain (this is a double plantain with the Latin name *Plantago major rosularis*, rather odd to look at, but interesting. I have great difficulty in growing it in the garden as I keep thinking it is a weed and digging it out!) Another handsome foliage for green arrangements is that of the August-flowering acanthus, with the lovely leaf that inspired the Greeks and was used in the design for the capitals of Corinthian columns. I find the leaves will last well if they are submerged in starch water overnight.

As all-green arrangements depend very much for their success on good shape, it is important to choose a vase that lends itself well to the creation of a flowing line. This is difficult in a conventional urn-shaped vase; on the other hand, the dolphin vase shown in my picture is particularly suitable for creating the left-sweeping curve of the two stems of Solomon's Seal which echoes the curve of the dolphin stem. The big hosta leaves on the right provide the necessary weight to the arrangement which otherwise would look very unbalanced. Green sedum heads, some flowers of green tobacco, two cream-edged hosta leaves and the pretty variegated leaf of the phlox Norah Leigh, right in the centre, complete the arrangement.

All-green arrangement

Clashing reds are wonderful this month as you have a wide choice of so many different shades in such flowers as gladioli, snapdragons, roses, dahlias, phlox and many more. Baskets look well filled with these annuals. If you use one with a handle, do not try to hide it: a handle is not necessary of course, but it is nice to let one show for a change. To hold the water, use any kind of ovenware dish, because you will not be able to see it in any case.

Grasses are beautiful, but you have to take care to arrange them in a way that will show off their delicate features. The illustration shows a group of grasses in a simple wine glass. Here the real difficulty is to avoid showing the wire netting, and this is done by placing two layers of wire over the top of the glass, and very carefully hooking them over the sides. As grass stems are very thin, it is easier to take a few in a bundle and place them in the vase together, holding the first little

Grasses in wine glass

Dahlias and branch in paper-covered tin

collection in place with one hand while you put in the next lot. As the glass is filled, you will find that they balance each other.

Arrangements for August

The simple arrangements for August are both oriental in mood—hence their simplicity. In one, the container is a tin covered with a rush paper, and in the second I have used an inexpensive oriental white china vase. When arranging a few flowers, it is more effective to use an uneven number—three, five or seven. In the first picture, I have used three dahlias; their rounded shape and brilliant colouring contrasts beautifully with the well-bleached branches of the sort you can usually find in any hedgerow or, better still, on the beach in summer.

The three tall flowers in the second arrangement are a campanula

63

called *C. pyramidalis*, which is a superb cut flower. I had this arrangement in the house for three weeks after it had been photographed, and all I did to it was to remove each flower bell as it faded and keep the container filled with water. This is a very important point: in summer one loses a lot of water through evaporation, and in winter much the same thing happens if you have central heating.

Campanulas and hosta leaves

Method: Place a little circle of rolled plasticine under a pin-holder and press firmly into position while the vase is dry—it will not adhere to a damp surface. Put in the tallest stem and the other two each side, then make a cluster of hosta leaves at the base.

Idea for the month

More about drying: this time preserving seed heads. I am often asked why one should take the trouble to dry by hanging the stem upside down when the seed heads will soon be dry on the plant. Well quite simply, if you pick the seed heads while they are still green and hang them heads down, all the sap runs down and when completely dry they are not nearly so brittle, so it is worth while. Do not tie too many stalks in one bundle, for the more the air can circulate the better they will dry, and don't forget to remove any leaves. Here are some good seed heads to look for:

Seed heads for hanging

from the hedgerow: dock, Old man's beard, plantain, hemlock.
from the vegetable garden: brussels sprouts in seed head, carrots, parsnips, leeks—all in seed head.
from the garden: hollyhock, foxglove, columbine, artemisia, delphinium, Lamb's ear (*Stachys lanata*) flower head, lupin, sedum (flower head), yellow yarrow (achillea).
To improve the colour of any yellow achillea dried in this way, first dip each head in borax.

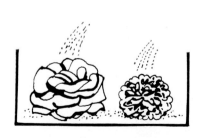

Delphinium heads drying   U.S. method of drying

There are a few flower heads that I have found dry better in a little water: achillea (the yellow heads keep their shape if dried in this way); hydrangea heads (pick these only when the colour is changing from blue to green or pink to red); hosta seed head (this method allows them to burst open and retain their seeds); and *Molucella laevis* (Bells of Ireland).

Apart from the above blooms, drying actual flower heads for colour needs a special technique. If you hang the heads of delphiniums upside down when they are in full flower, there is a good chance that they will dry well; larkspur can be dried in the same way. But generally speaking the only way to achieve good results in drying flower heads is to use the American method, which works well, for instance, with open roses, dahlias, pansies, passion flowers and dogwood flowers. However, it is very expensive. You need a box large enough to hold the flowers, complete with stalks, and a little deeper than your largest flower head. Shake a layer of borax or, better still, silica gel to cover the bottom of the box. Lay in the blooms face up, having removed the stems and inserted wire in their place (stems always break off in the treatment). Gently shake in enough powder to cover the whole bloom and then leave the box in a warm room for two to three days. Test for dryness by scraping away a little of the powder to see if the petals are crisp. One big snag to this method is that the flowers all need to be kept in constant dry heat or they quickly lose their colour. The resulting flower heads are useful for vases in a permanently heated room, and they can look lovely arranged under a glass dome.

September

⪼⪼⪼⪼⪼⪼⪼⪼⪼⪼⪼⪼⪼⪼⪼⪼⪼⪼⪼⪼⪼⪼⪼⪼⪼⪼⪼⪼⪼⪼⪼⪼⪼⪼⪼

Bonfire smoke seems to hang in the air, and with heavy dews and falling apples there is a feeling of autumn approaching. At this time of year in the old days I loved to visit Sheffield park and walk at the end of the lake along a border of Michaelmas daisies edged with blue gentians— a really beautiful sight. Now, with lack of help, these flowers will soon fade from popularity, as gardens today have to be easily managed, and more and more the cry is for shrubs and roses. So, sadly, these memories of hazy blues in the smokey September light are things of the past. However, to compensate, one is able to enjoy the block of colour that a bank of hydrangea will give, and nothing could be more easily kept: they need only plenty of manure and, in a dry season, extra water, which seems little enough to ask when you can have a mass of bloom for over three months in the year.

This is the season for berries, and you might like to make one of the cones I suggested for July (see page 57) covered this time with fruits and berries. Use hips and blackberries picked from the hedges and to these add perhaps small green grapes that are very inexpensive this month, crab apples and plums from the garden, and finally tuck in a few red roses to give a touch of luxury.

With harvest festival in mind, try arranging fruit and flowers together. Take a low dish and fill it with a piece of Oasis and wire netting, tied securely with a piece of string—this is important because fruit is heavy and it can overbalance the dish very easily. Select some rosy apples, plums and a peach or two, and a nice bunch of grapes. Peppers and onions can be used too, to add a good touch of colour and texture. Collect some sprays of berries, coloured foliage, seed heads of sweet corn or foxgloves to give you a nice point for the top, and sprays of Old Man's Beard to fall gracefully over the front. Start as always three-quarters of the

67

way back in the vase, and put in your tall seed head and coloured foliage; then place the fruit: apples can be impaled with cocktail sticks into the Oasis to prevent them from falling off. Finally, to give more colour add one or two open roses or a few dahlias.

Arrangement for September

The photograph for this month shows a copper jug filled with berries and fruits.

Berries etc. in copper jug

Method: Place a piece of crushed wire into the jug. You should aim to fill the jug with wire from the bottom right up to the top, and then take a snag end of wire and just hook it over the top of the vase to prevent the wire getting all pushed down to the bottom of the jug. You will

68

see here that I have followed the curve of the jug handle in placing the branches. When you have a lovely jug like this, try to use its shape in making your arrangement.

Idea for the month

September is a good time to choose material for pressing. Bracken and turning beech sprays, single leaves of horse chestnut and maple all press well. They will add colour to any dried or partly dried arrangement that you may want to make in winter. As the single leaves will lose their stems when pressed, you will have to attach a false stem to each when you remove it from the paper. False stems are quite easy to make, using florist's wire covered in brown crêpe paper: buy a packet of the paper and, without opening it, cut through all the layers at once at half-inch

Making a false stem for leaf

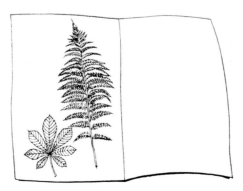

Pressing ferns, horse chestnut

69

intervals. This will give you a large number of strips of the right width and manageable length. Then cut your wire into pieces of suitable length and cover each with paper, winding the strip round the wire at an angle and stretching it as you go to keep it taut. I find it helps to fix one end of the paper with a dab of glue before starting to wind, and another dab of glue will hold it firm when you have finished the stem. Place it at the back of the leaf, stick it over with Sellotape, and to make sure it stays firm, wind it round the stump of the leaf stem as shown in the drawing.

To press ferns and sprays, lay them between layers of newspaper and put them under the carpet or a pile of books for two or three days. If you use blotting paper it may give you a better colour, but I feel it is hardly worth the additional cost.

October

Autumn is really here! This season brings wonderful colour to the leaves of trees and shrubs, one or two of which, like the Guelder Rose (*Viburnum opulus sterile*), also known as the Snowball Tree, have leaves that will stand well in water in all their lovely red colours. Branches of azaleas also last well, though these plants are so precious that you have to need a small piece very badly, for in cutting it you will destroy next year's bloom. The reason that leaves and branches of autumn colour just curl up as soon as they come into the house is simply because the change in leaf colour is part of the plant's slowing-down process, which you have no doubt learnt all about at school; and as the sap is not now rising fast, a cut branch cannot take up water quickly enough to prevent the leaves from curling through lack of moisture. It is naturally tempting to pick branches of these brilliant-coloured leaves, and I sometimes do so for special occasions, knowing that it is for the glory of a day. But do avoid picking from any rare shrub, for it is such a waste to pick a branch that may have taken years to grow.

The last of the dahlias usually flower in October, and you must enjoy each and every one as any day now we may have a frost. I pick continually, and often find that I have more flowers in the house than during any other month.

Garden chrysanthemums and all the October seed heads seem to go so well together. Now that we have chrysanthemums in the shops all the year round, the joy of picking a fresh bloom with that lovely stringent tangy smell on a crisp autumn morning, has alas gone for ever. I do not like the varieties with the really gigantic blooms, though they are a source of pride to the grower, and I still much prefer the single varieties. These are very effective when they are grown commercially, and the American-spray type with their wide colour range are of course a

71

Autumn crocus in silver dish

Planting bulbs in fibre

wonderful buy, not only for us but also for the florists, as they really do last, and this is of course very important. So I do appreciate their merits: it is simply that I find I get tired of a good thing when I have it through every month of the year!

Arrangement for October

The photograph for this month shows a silver dish with an arrangement of five flowers—the giant white autumn crocus. The silvery foliage of cineraria shows off the pure white of the crocus. This is an excellent example of the use of grey foliage in flower arrangement.

Among grey-leaved plants which you can grow for flower arranging, I can thoroughly recommend artemisia in all its varieties, the cineraria of the illustration (its proper name is *Senecio maritima*), *Onopordon acanthium* or Scots Thistle, *Senecio laxifolius*, a very good small shrub with grey-backed leaves that are useful all the year round, *Stachys lanata* or Lamb's Ears and *Verbascum broussa*, which is a good grey form of the common mullein. These leaves can be used as a foil for colour—grey and pink, grey with blues and mauves—and they always make excellent background material.

Idea for the month

Bulbs should be planted in pots for early spring flowering. They take fifteen weeks from planting to blooming, so this will give you a guide about when to expect results. What are called prepared hyacinths have been specially chilled and are more reliable if you want really early bulbs for Christmas. Roman hyacinths force well and easily and usually you can rely on having a bowl in bloom on Christmas morning. The multiflora hyacinths are a good buy and give you several heads on one bulb.

Hyacinths are best planted in bulb fibre, which you buy in bags from any seedsman or garden shop. All you have to do is to soak it well, squeeze out any surplus water, put a good layer in the bottom of a bowl, place in the bulbs closely but not touching and cover with more fibre leaving just the tip of the bulbs showing. Then either wrap the bowl in newspaper, bury it completely in a bed of ashes outside, and bring it in after a few weeks; or keep the bowl in the dark and water daily until the shoots are well up, when it can be brought into a room. I often simply keep my bowls in a dark cupboard all the time.

Crocus are very effective when grown just in shingle. Plant them in the same way, water lightly, and leave them in the dark for six weeks or until the shoots are well up; then bring them into the sitting-room and water freely. The shingle gives a pleasing effect so that you see them as if they were growing in a river bed. You can grow "Geranium" narcissi in the same way, or an early variety called "Paper White", but though these are beautiful in the early stages, as they flower they have to be staked and this is rather difficult. With crocus, of course, this is no problem.

Bulb glass

I still get a childish delight from watching a hyacinth grow in a bulb glass! You can get these from seedsmen and garden shops for very little, and as you can see from the drawing, they allow you to watch the roots developing as well as the flower. Bulbs grown in this way usually develop much more quickly than when using other methods, so you can race the rest of the family if they are growing theirs in fibre. Bulb glasses look attractive all the time, and one or a pair on the mantelpiece will give you something of interest to watch for fourteen weeks or more.

November

I think that a combination of dried and fresh flowers give a more pleasing effect than an all-dried vase. I first used dried arrangements many years ago, when working on flower decorations in flats and houses in London. During the autumn I would add seed heads and flower spikes that gradually dried off in the water, and I was often asked just to bring along something to add to what was still quite a pretty arrangement. By adding a few dried pieces to give colour, such as yellow achilleas or heads of well-coloured hydrangea, this became quite naturally a dried group.

Arrangement for November

The arrangement in a Victorian metal and china vase is just the sort of group of mixed fresh and dried flowers that I have been describing. Branches of glycerined lime outline the shape, which is filled in with dried grasses, Bells of Ireland stems, dock seed-heads, dried hydrangea and a magnificent lily seed-head in the centre. Then I added seven apricot-coloured chrysanthemums, and for their sake I have filled the vase with water in the ordinary way. Although this means that the dried stems go soggy at the ends, they soon dry off and can be used again. However, if you want to avoid this happening, you can do so by using a splendid invention called a flower pick, which is a little tube rather like a test-tube with a spike at the end which will sit in the Oasis, and filled with water will hold enough for one flower. Flower picks can be bought at a florist shop, or you can make your own using a small test-tube of the kind you can get for children's chemistry sets though, since these have no spikes, of course, you will have to make little holes in the Oasis to receive them.

75

Fresh and dried flowers

Pressed flowers for table mat, door plate

Idea for the month

The time has come to give you some more ideas for using the flowers and leaves you have pressed and dried during the summer and autumn. The illustrations show you some ideas that I think would make attractive Christmas presents.

My first suggestion is for making table mats. For these you need some sheets of stiff artist's paper of the kind you can get at large stationers and art shops, in suitable background colours: dusky blue, dull red and lime green are all good. For the mat tops you can buy round glass mats from big stores or, as these may become rather expensive, you can get some pieces of clear perspex from a do-it-yourself shop. I find pieces about

77

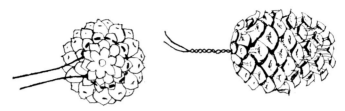

Wiring a pine cone

8 by 9 inches the best, and this size is good for making pictures too. You must also have some upholstery braid.

Using your glass or perspex mats as patterns, cut pieces of coloured paper of the same size. Arrange your flowers on them, and when you are happy with the designs, glue the flowers into place by lifting each one in turn and carefully spreading a very little Uhu gum on the back before lightly pressing it into position on the paper again. Be careful not to use too much glue and allow a little time for it to dry. Then cover the arrangement with any scrap of paper and press it under a book for a few hours before finally placing the glass on top. To finish off stick a length of upholstery braid round the mat, turning it over both above and below and overlapping it a trifle at the ends.

Pictures are made in the same way, with the addition of a little loop on the back for hanging. Door finger-plates, as in the photograph, are also popular, especially since these can now be found in perspex at large department stores.

A dried-flower ball hung on a ribbon makes another charming Christmas present, and also sells wonderfully at bazaars or bring-and-buy sales. As a base you will need a little ball of Styrofoam or other suitable material, and whenever possible you should use flowers and seed-heads that still have firm stems even after drying. Push the stalks into the ball until it is completely covered and then tie on a ribbon loop. Poppy seed heads, pieces of yellow achillea, helichrysums, lavender and statice are all good for this idea. Small pine cones can be used too, but these will have to be provided with a stem: take a piece of florist's wire, bend it into a shape like a hairpin and thread it into the cone, just above the base, pulling it in gently until the loop is hidden under the scales. Then bring the two ends of the wire together and twist them into a stem as shown in the drawing.

December

It is a constant delight to me that daffodils are in the shops again this month, and so we have come full circle! Anemones are in good supply and would look particularly cheerful arranged in a painted box, as I described for February. These are among the few flowers that really seem to dislike Oasis, so you should use only wire netting when arranging them. When you buy a bunch, take out all the red and purple shades for your box arrangement, keeping back any white flowers: these can be used for another vase with a little greenery from the garden, and you will then have two arrangements for the price of one.

Winter greens can be quite inspiring: try arranging the yellow-spotted laurel (aucuba) with some dried ferns, yellow-leaved privet (although it will have started to die back at this time, it is surprising how long it keeps its leaves) and bergenia—even when picked on the frostiest morning, these leaves revive in warm water in no time at all. A head of rhododendron leaves makes a very good centre. Winter evergreens are rather heavy, but the fern and one or two stems of glycerined beech or lime flowers will give your arrangement a wonderful feeling of lightness. And perhaps you can afford to buy some lovely eucalyptus leaves, which have a good grey colour and fall naturally in graceful curves when arranged. Not only do eucalyptus leaves last very well in water: they also take up glycerine well, giving you another form in which to use them.

Ideas for Christmas decorations

Evergreens make lovely garlands, wreaths for door knockers and so on. Berried holly is sometimes hard to get, and so you may have to buy some artificial berries and wire them on. To make a garland, the simplest way is to bind small pieces of mixed evergreen on to thick string or sheets of rolled newspaper. Cut pieces three to four inches long of as many different kinds of evergreen as you can get—box, yew, golden

Making a garland

cypress, variegated and green holly—but avoid privet and ivy as these shrivel quickly out of water. Keep the different varieties in separate piles and if you have no berried holly make one pile of hips, cotoneaster berries or even bows of red ribbon to produce a little colour. Bind one piece of evergreen into position at a time by holding the string and branch in your left hand and, with your right hand, winding fine wire or thin string round them in a figure of eight, as shown in the drawings. Use different pieces of green in rotation so that you don't get too many of one kind of foliage together, and wire on berries if necessary to any suitable dark green leaves. If you want to make a lot of garlands, get several people to help; then each of you can do a length and they can all be fixed together later. These garlands can be hung round or across a room, round the pillars in a church, round a mantelpiece or over a doorway.

To make a fresh garland for the door, the principle is very much the same. For the base, use a wire coat hanger pulled open to make a circle, and on to this bind either holly alone or mixed evergreens as before. Finally, as shown in the drawing, tie on a large bow of red ribbon with ends hanging down the centre.

Making a door garland

Metal hangers are used for my next suggestion too: you will need two of them, and you should bind each one with crêpe paper cut into strips as I described on page 69. I think that red or gold are the most effective colours to use for this. After binding them, tie together the straight sides of the hangers as shown, and either hang one or two baubles from each of the hooks and finish off with a bunch of mistletoe and ribbon bows; or, as shown in the drawing, bind on some mixed evergreens (the crêpe paper covering means that it will not matter if bits of the hangers show through), add a few baubles and a bow and hang it all up by a wire loop slipped through the upper end.

Wooden coat hangers also make good foundations for Christmas decorations. Bind two of them, again with crêpe paper or with evergreens

Joining two coat hangers   Decorating coat hangers

F

as for making garlands, then cross the hangers at right angles with the upper edges together, tying the centre of each hanger to the hook of the other. Hang a bunch of bells or baubles from one hook, together with ribbon bows, and you will have a pretty decoration to suspend by the other hook from the light in the centre of a room.

You can have a lot of fun with a wide range of shapes and cut-outs in a hard and water-resistant form of Oasis called Styrofoam. Try making the large round balls into miniature holly trees: stick pieces of holly into the ball and add bows of red ribbon and clusters of berries; then push a short length of bamboo cane into the ball and with plasticine or Polyfilla fix a small white-painted flower pot to the other end.

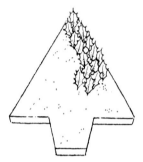

Polystyrene Christmas tree

Cut a shape as shown in the drawing from a polystyrene tile to make a flat formal tree. Cover with individual holly leaves (variegated are best) by pressing each into place with a pin, and finish with berry clusters or ribbon bows. Of course you can use this material to make more ambitious shapes or even whole scenes—perhaps a nativity or a reindeer and coach—which you can fix to the wall. I find it easier to cut the polystyrene with either a hot knife or one with a saw edge; and I understand one can buy a battery-heated wire device which cuts through it very easily.

Big balls made out of tissue paper are another pretty decoration. For these you can use white paper, putting a little clear gum along the edges and sprinkling on glitter while it is still wet; or you can use red tissue, which will look more effective if you have three or four shades of red paper. Cut the sheets in half by slitting the whole packet, then trim to a wavy edge on both sides. Add glitter at this stage if you want it, then gather each sheet in the middle by ruckling it into your hand and securing it with a wire, the ends of which can be used to wire the gathered sheet into a ball (an apple will do quite well, but naturally does not last very long). Continue to wire in your gathered pieces of paper until the ball is entirely covered. Then hang it up or make it into a tree as shown in the drawing.

Paper decorations   Paper bobble and tree

Then, of course, there is paint and glitter for twigs and evergreens. When using a gold or silver aerosol spray, don't cover all the material solidly: it is so much more effective if you just run the spray over lightly. If you want to get a sparkling effect, dust the branches with glitter while they are still wet (one point to remember here is that you should always spread fresh newspaper on the floor before you glitter: then when you have finished you can pick the paper up, shake all the glitter into a bowl and use it again. If you keep the same newspaper that you used when spraying on the paint, all your extra glitter will stick to the paint and be lost).

A lovely feeling of frost can be created by painting clear gum on bare branches or evergreen leaves and then sprinkling heavily with glass glitter (this can be bought from the Constance Spry shops or from Tyllier of Woodstock Street, London, W.1). Small pieces of glittered ivy and holly can be used to make a pretty table centre: from a florist's buy a round Oasis holder complete with Oasis, cut a small circle out of the centre of the Oasis, insert a candle, surround it with your glittered twigs and finish with ribbon bows.

For the Christmas table, nothing looks prettier than candles. Buy a cake board from Woolworths, and cover it with some foil or gay shiny paper (Paper Chase in Tottenham Court Road in London have a wonderful choice of papers). On this put a mound made of plasticine or alabastine (though with the latter you have to work fast as it sets so quickly) and into it press the candle, ribbon bows and fresh berried holly.

Large church candles used in this way look very good particularly if they are placed on a table-cloth or runner made from tarlatan—the fine material used for ballet skirts. On to this, using a transparent gum, you can stick shapes cut from coloured felts, ribbons or flock paper: formal Christmas trees or peals of bells or even whole Christmas scenes complete with sleighs. A cloth decorated like this adds a very Christmassy touch even if as a centrepiece you have just fruit and crackers.

Tree on cloth

Note on Growers and Seedsmen

If you have difficulty in finding seeds or plants of some of the more unusual flowers I have mentioned in this book—or that you have heard about and want to grow—I would heartily recommend, for plants, Bressingham Gardens in Diss, Norfolk; and for seeds, Thompson and Morgan of Ipswich, Suffolk, and Suttons of Reading in Berkshire. E. B. le Grice of Roseland Nurseries, Yarmouth Road, North Walsham in Norfolk, and the Albrighton Rose Nurseries, of Albrighton, near Wolverhampton, both grow unusual roses.